40x41

"Don't be too timid and squeamish about your actions. All life is an experiment. The more experiments you make the better."

Ralph Waldo Emerson

# 40x41: Midlife Crisis Postponed

G^eo^ Davis

Essex Editions

Copyright © 2016 by G^eo^ Davis

All rights reserved. No part of this book may be reproduced or transmitted in any form or by any means, electronic or mechanical, including photocopying, recording or by any information storage and retrieval system, without written permission from the publisher, except for the inclusion of brief quotations in a review.

Published in the United States by Essex Editions.

ISBN-10:0-9967870-2-X
ISBN-13:978-0-9967870-2-4

Essex Editions
Post Office Box 25
Essex, New York 12936
www.essexeditions.com
contact@essexeditions.com

For Susan Bacot-Davis,
my Maasai bride

## Contents

| | |
|---|---|
| INTRODUCTION | 1 |
| Midlife Crisis Postponed | 2 |
| El Miedo Paraliza | 3 |
| Mission Reboot | 4 |
| Split Sprouts | 6 |
| Moribundignant | 7 |
| Box of Time | 8 |
| On Turning Forty | 9 |
| Cardinal Rule | 12 |
| Caveat | 13 |
| A Witty Saying | 14 |
| 12 Steps: A Minifesto | 15 |
| Tele Time | 20 |
| Mobile Midlife | 21 |
| Contours & Artifacts | 22 |
| Cracked | 23 |
| Climb, Drip, Climb | 25 |
| Roman Shades | 26 |
| Second Hand | 27 |
| Fountain of Fading Youth | 28 |
| Recycling | 29 |
| Sound Escape | 30 |
| Lunar Cycle | 31 |
| Desiderata | 32 |
| Prime Pulp | 33 |
| Calypso | 34 |
| Walkabout | 35 |
| Chiaroscuro | 36 |

| | |
|---|---|
| Protean | 37 |
| Twitch | 38 |
| Fall Flutter | 40 |
| Midlife Midwife I | 41 |
| Free Heeling | 42 |
| Italic | 43 |
| Paris Time | 44 |
| Paris by Night | 45 |
| Ink and Trinket | 46 |
| Handmade Notes | 47 |
| New Growth | 49 |
| Slurp | 50 |
| Portage | 51 |
| Speed Trap I | 52 |
| Seatless Cycles | 54 |
| Drift | 55 |
| Cuckold Moon | 56 |
| Paper Poem | 57 |
| Handmade Healing | 58 |
| Hazmat | 59 |
| Phototoxic | 60 |
| Scream | 61 |
| Spring | 62 |
| Poetic Divagation | 63 |
| Like a Lichen | 64 |
| Wonder | 65 |
| Living Fossils | 67 |
| Benign | 68 |
| Railyard Hobo | 70 |

| | |
|---|---|
| Crepusculum | 71 |
| Design Shoal | 72 |
| Blame-ology | 73 |
| Dance | 75 |
| Dance Trance | 76 |
| To Cycle | 78 |
| Coffee Ring | 79 |
| Rupture Relief | 80 |
| Hernia | 81 |
| Riding the Wave | 88 |
| To Invent this Morning | 89 |
| Canine Time | 90 |
| Making Love | 91 |
| Soar | 92 |
| Palavering | 93 |
| Searching | 94 |
| Daily Compost | 95 |
| Pickup Lines | 96 |
| Ode to Siri, Interrupted | 97 |
| What Will You Do? | 100 |
| Autodidact, or Find Your Why | 101 |
| Historic | 104 |
| Ellipsis | 105 |
| Fossil | 106 |
| POSTSCRIPT | 107 |
| ACKNOWLEDGEMENTS | 109 |

## Introduction

This is a meditation. A poetry cycle. A lyric essay. A doodle diary. A scrapbook. A remix.

This is the first foray into middle age lived inside out, a journey with blurry borders and objectives, an open notebook spilling artifacts and tattered pages, an evolving (and frequently fumbling) documentary about the midlife transition. Mine. Yours?

This is an attempt—fueled with curiosity, stubborn optimism, and a twinge of desperation—to eschew a midlife crisis for a midlife leap. This is a sketch, perhaps a caricature, of trying and failing and trying again. This is the detritus of middle age recycled into song; sewn into a patchwork cape; cut into strips, dredged in paste, and papier-mâchéd into an oracle. Or a piñata.

This is midlife.

G<sup>eo</sup> Davis

# Midlife Crisis Postponed

The dusty caboose
of my fourth decade
lumbers closer, closer.
Hobo instincts flutter.
Pack light. Jog alongside.
Jump aboard. Stow away.
Still. Stillness in motion.

I resist; the urge subsides.
The caboose rumbles past.
Silent. Silence. Solitude.
A flicker of adrenaline.

What if I could overcome
debilitating bugaboos
and bust forty's balls?
Vanquish the to do list,
purge my doughy paunch
(literal and figurative),
de-quarantine the drafts,
indulge my latent doodler,
transform the next decade
into a parade of firsts
and at lasts... What if?

I can. I must. I will.
This is my scrapbook,
This is my chronicle.

# El Miedo Paraliza

# Mission Reboot

By twenty I'd be a poet.
By thirty, a novelist.
By forty, a memoirist.

Perhaps a decade later
I'd expire telling stories
by a babbling brook
with a smoldering fire
and a jug of wine.

At thirty nine I took inventory.
The workbench was sow backed
but the warehouse was bare.
Exotic souvenirs camouflaged
scaling, yellowing to do lists.
A weathered leathered inbox
towered toward toppling;
a yawning outbox
casketed a fossil fly.

Forty trudged closer.

I removed myself
for a windy, lonely,
and monkish month
at the folded edge
of the dusty desert

and the muddy Chama
to untangle tales for
magpies and coyotes.

Beginnings are easy.
Endings are difficult.
Start in the middle.
Last chance.
Mission reboot.

# Split Sprouts

## Moribundignant

The dead heaviest
I'd ever, ever been.
Paunchy two fifteen.
Pounds, not o'clock.

Belly fat, jowl fat,
brain fat, will fat.
Distorted, plumped,
stalled, and stumped.

How did it happen?
When did it happen?
What, where and how
from here? From now!

# Box of Time

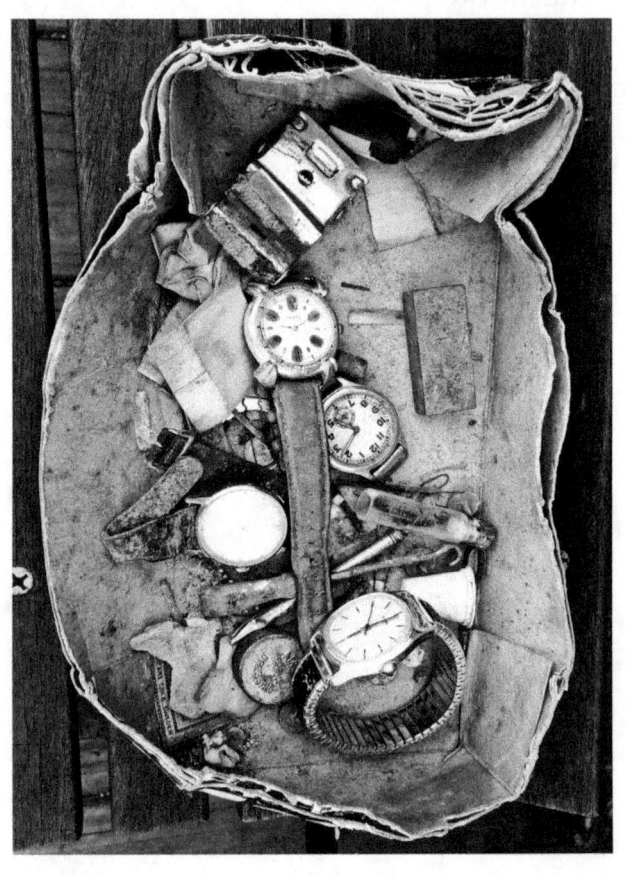

# On Turning Forty

I.

"This is it," my father sighed when he turned forty.

"This is it," he repeated throughout the next decade.

I wondered if this it was hardwired, if it was in my DNA.

I decided it wasn't. No it for me. Fast track the adventure.

II.

When I turned thirty-nine I confirmed that this wasn't it, this story, this race to live a life before it's stolen. Or surrendered.

I almost liked thirty nine. The most voluptuous prime number multiplied in a mirror. There was vanity in it—puffed up and flouncy—but beauty too. A sort of balance. A law of nature. Of physics and mathematics.

I rolled the digits around with my tongue and scrawled three nine in loose, inky swirls wondering secretly if my indulgence was just the calm before the storm.

III.

Forty brought floods and burst pipes. Metaphorical baptisms. Learning to swim by drowning.

It was a year of gastrointestinal tests, my viscera protesting my favorite victuals. Cashews, pistachios, peas. Milk and cheese and yogurt. Turns out curds and whey are not just children's rhyme filler. Lactose and casein are gut busters for me. Ditto wheat, barley, gluten, the very building blocks of bread and beer and basic boy joys. Turns out that meat, fish and veggies are my gutsy gastronomic gang.

It was a year of biking and gyming. I lashed my laptop to the elliptical machine, the recumbent bike, the windsurfers. No, not the windsurfers. I acquired a tolerance for chia seeds and spirulina smoothies. I cleansed. I energized. I shrank.

IV.

Lard clings to my jelly belly and assimus maximus, but melts away elsewhere.
Bullshit! It doesn't melt. That's poet talk, and yesterday's wine is tomorrow's vinegar. Melts becomes drips becomes oozes becomes slippery.

"Pare away pretty poetry," I beg my puffed up parody in the mirror. "Stand up straight. Drop the mask. Shed the costume. Lose the skin of the lion…"

If thirty nine was tumescent narcissism, forty is the fork in the proverbial road. It's a choice. A collection of angles, or a bulging belly? Sparse precision or bloat?

This is NOT it. This is the story. This is the adventure. This is the end of the beginning.

# Cardinal Rule

# Caveat

This is not
a memoir,
a poem,
a story,
an apology,
or an excuse
for you to spend
your hard earned,
begged, borrowed, stolen
ducats on ersatz escapism
or saccharine wonderlands.
No adorable moral gift bag.
No pimped out pocket rocket.
No selective serotonin reuptake
inhibitors, erectile dysfunction tips,
or magic carpet rides to the front steps
of your posh brownstone, permission slip
pinned to your pima, wine-dyed tuxedo shirt.
No stain eraser for three shades of lipstick
graffitied across your cheek, your collar
to ensure that you're welcomed home
with open arms, a tender kiss, and
a hushed, "I missed you, dear."
No, this is not.

# A Witty Saying

# 12 Steps: A Minifesto

1.

Fat to fit by forty.
Find an app for that.
Download it.
Plug in my data.
Make a goal.
Make a plan.
Make a sacrifice.
Day after day.

2.

Fuel right; feel right.
A nutrition test,
a blood letting,
a wondering wait,
a list of food fouls,
another pledge.
More sacrifice.

3.

Edit the maudlin hunch
that my forth decade
will be my final chapter,
a romantic curtain call.
Narrate a lean, inky map
for the next four decades.
Revise, re-plot, rewrite.

4.

Cut. Tighten. Simplify.
Words are my opium,
my Holy Grail, my
Dulcinea del Toboso.
Time to de-binge...
Stop hoarding.
Start purging.
Write lean.
Linguistic
liposuction.

5.

Swap paunch for poetry.
Replace forty pounds
with forty poems
and forty doodles
within one year.
No almosts.
No excuses.

6.

Wrangle storytelling
from interstices and
wrinkled arroyos,
dog-eared margins and
back alleys into the
light, onto center stage.

7.

Untether. Weigh anchor.
De-dock. De-harbor.
Embark. Errant.
Adventure.
Mobilize vagabondish.
Helm short-handed.
No mobile menagerie.
Rooted? Shed it!

8.

Fine-tune flânerie.
Wander. Wonder.
Discern and yield
to ebbs and flows.
Get seduced and
pulled off course
by possibility
time and again.

9.

Unfurl. Bloom.
Live inside out.
Admit failures.
Ditty, doodle,
and perambulate.
Own addiction
to marginalia.
Harness candor.

10.

Accept
assistance.
Scrum. Beta.
Launch fast.
Launch often.
Review in realtime,
at bedtime, all the time.
Finish. Celebrate.
Or pull the plug,
and restart.

11.

Open source.
Crowdsource.
Share ship's log.
Invite judgment.
Respect criticism
or accolades
without bias.
Warmly welcome
all sojourners.

12.

Twelve steps.
Twelve months.
Twelve hazards.
Twelve opportunities.
Recover. Discover. Repeat

# Tele Time

# Mobile Midlife

Dodgy doggerel and
digital detritus,
curious confections and
midlife mutterings,
why's and sighs, whines and signs,
cribbed, clipped, curated,
and collecting in my pocket.
So much battery fueled
psycho-spelunking and
belly button lint gazing
burbling and fermenting
with telephone numbers,
eager emails, ebooks, and
tomorrow's spring weather.

# Contours & Artifacts

# Cracked

"What's that?" my niece asks,
Running a razor thin fingernail
Down, up, down, up,
Tracing the laugh line
To the left of my mouth.

She asked the same question
Last summer when she was five.
I remind her, "It's a wrinkle."
"But, how did you get it?"

Same question, same wrinkle,
Same niece, same concern.
She's racing youth and winning.
She's poised and articulate
And funny and stubborn.
"What's this?" she asks. Again.

"It's a wrinkle," I explain again.
Her nail, no longer paper thin,
Still slices at my face as she runs
It along the folded flesh.
"It's a crack," she says. "Not a wrinkle."

"Or both," I say, gently moving her hand
From my face. "Wrinkles are like cracks."
"But how could you crack your face?"
"Laughing," I say. "And smiling."
She pulls a queer, incredulous look

And shakes her head, side-to-side.
"No, smiling can't crack your face."
I show her my asymmetrical smile,
Run my own index finger along the wrinkle.
"Oh," she says touching to her own face.
She smiles, laughs, feels for wrinkles.

"I don't have any cracks on my face."

# Climb, Drip, Climb

# Roman Shades

"But why," I ask,
"Must the curtains
fly at half mast?"
"Because," she sighs,
"they must. Or else
the silk will crush."
So I leave them,
droopy eyelids
veiling the view.

# Second Hand

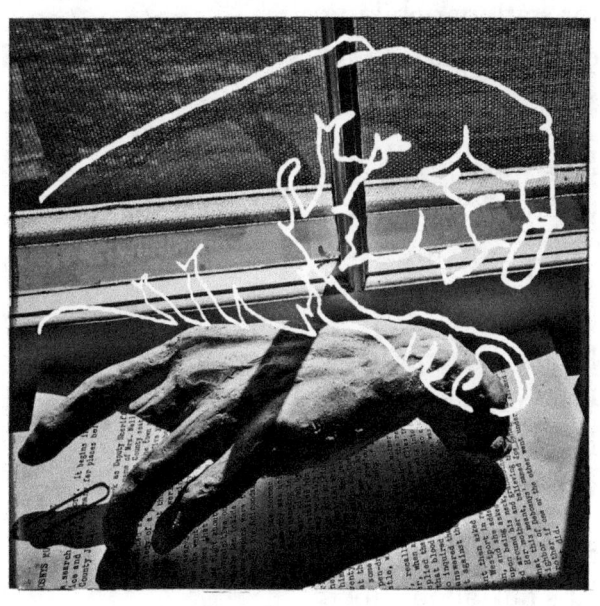

# Fountain of Fading Youth

There will be days
for telemark turns,
Nordic kick glides,
and windsurfing jibes.

There will be others
for stationary biking,
elliptical machining,
stretches and crunches.

But, the doc says,
when stuck at your desk,
clench and unclench
your stomach and butt.

Drink lots of water.
It'll make you pee.
For to pee, you see,
will make you move.

Speaking of movement
let's talk about fiber.
Are you getting enough?
Bran? Psyllium husk?

Take Omega-3,
vitamins B, C and D,
and lather on sunscreen,
or you'll look like me.

# Recycling

# Sound Escape

A chainsaw whines and screams and subsides, only to whine again a few minutes later. Angry. Testy. Persistent. Like a two year old throwing a tantrum.

Closer, outside my window, chimes cling and clong in the shade of an immense ginkgo tree.

I try to organize my thoughts in digital scrawl, postulating, developing, concluding. Posting and re-posting. Whine. Cling. Scream. Clong.

A garbage truck thunders past, doubling the thirty-mile per hour speed limit. Then a slow car. And another. Then quiet except for the crinkle-strain-crinkle-strain of the palm paddles on the ceiling fan above my head. Type. Click, click, click.

The ferry arrives, reverses its rumbling engines to brake momentum, then glides into the dock to disgorge a parade of cars, trucks and motorcycles. Ignitions whir and catch. Engines purr or growl. Some cough. A horn bids welcome or farewell. A seagull responds.

Think. Type. Post.

# Lunar Cycle

# Desiderata

Early mornings
Velvet winter
Sunny slopes
Playful bride
Ample walkabout
Precocious spring
Fertile flow
Sumptuous sunrise
Eternal cyclabouts
Taffy byways
Kinful summer
Robust gardens
Languid waters
Vibrant autumn
Scudding seas
Concluded stories

# Prime Pulp

# Calypso

When thirty nine sashayed in with her bodacious tatas and voluptuous curves I panicked.

My dormant radar quivered to life. "Beware: Temptation," flashed the neon pulse.

And I knew. Heed not Calypso's hypnotic hips and waspy midriff, those painted lips, that coquettish paisley smile, her saccharine song. I knew it was a trap.

In less than a year forty would appear where thirty nine had stood, all angles and paunch, arms crossed and steely glare.

No, forty would not be so sexy sweet. Not by far.

Beyond the horizon I'd heard the fleshy sixties offered some latter day rewards, but the forties and fifties? Twice Calypsoed. A double header. A score ashore a hoary moor for sure!

No. When thirty nine sashayed in I dug deep and stayed my course.

# Walkabout

# Chiaroscuro

We paint ourselves into corners,
shady, feverish, asphyxiating corners,
where we pace and gasp for breath.
A single bulb dangles between us.
A crumpled map and a pair of glasses
drown in a puddle of light on the table.
A chair askew between light and shadows,
another tipped over backward where it fell,
clatter still lingering, temper's testament.

# Protean

# Twitch

I have a twitch beneath my right eye. In reflection it's my left eye, or so it seems when I shave or glance in the rearview mirror to check for spinach in my teeth. The not-so-subtle pulse flutters just above the cheekbone in my eye socket.

I wonder if anyone ever called me a twitch when I was a boy, like maybe Henry, my brother's godfather, who asked my mother if I was hyperactive three dozen years ago when he visited us with his pipe and sweater and tweed blazer and gentle, considered phrases.

ADHD today, or maybe just ADD, but a twitch back in 1975. And a twitch again today, but just a small twitch like a miniature heart beating in plain view to remind me I'm alive. I'm alive. I'm alive.

The French touch an index finger to the exact place where my miniature heart trembles. Sometimes they pull down the lower eyelid slightly and say, "Mon œil!" to express disbelief. We say, "My foot!"

But back to the twitch. It arrived just before my fortieth birthday like a membership letter in junior AARP. A reminder to get more sleep. Or wear sunglasses. Or turn off the computer.

"It's a tick," you tell me, "Not a twitch. And it's temporary, like dark bags under your eyes."

Yes, but it endures. I wonder if anyone ever called an enduring tick a twitch.

# Fall Flutter

# Midlife Midwife I

*That damned telephone,*
*my bride declares,*
*is your mistress, your...*
*your mobile paramour,*
*the object of your desires*
*and confessions, your*
*most intimate moments,*
*and lusty caresses.*

No, no, I say again
and again and again.
She's not. It's not.
And I think but don't say,
anyway she's more midwife
than lascivious lover.
She holds my quivering
hand, reminds me to
wake, breath, push, rest
as I muddle my way
through this eternal
gestation toward the
possibility of nascence.

# Free Heeling

## Italic

I lean into the page,
wind at my back,
eyes on the prize,
dreaming of tango.

I'm moving now,
almost falling down
but no, not quite,
just falling forward,
headlong toward
my emphatic point
pressed earnestly in-
to and through type.

Pedal to the mettle.
Stop. Go. No typo.
Race over. Stand up.
Straight. Still. Again.

# Paris Time

# Paris by Night

Think back, you self aggrandizing dilettante, that's you at thirty, still fleeing the flinty face of commitment, still chasing mysteries and searching for answers to questions long forgotten.

For what?

Tickled by musky curls of an armpit you don't recognize in the darkness, her so recently exotic portrait and story and dance consumed by you while sirens Dopple.

Perhaps we all live in darkness, drawn to the flicker of light emanating from a fading affair, vagrants bumping clumsily, intentionally, hungrily in a Paris night.

# Ink and Trinket

# Handmade Notes

This is no sentimental eulogy,
for loose leaf and Moleskines
lead pencils and India ink.
Not a Luddite manifesto,
nor a digital doomsday,
but I am jotting notes,
and stuffing them in
a box, just in case.

This is a tribute to
smudged postcards and
illustrated napkins, to
inky, crinkly Air Mailers,
fridge door Post-Its, and
tattooed scraps passed
hand-to-hand in class.

Don't get me wrong.
Vmail and email,
texts and tweets,
check-ins and photos
have swell roles to play.

But handmade notes,
smudged and fading,
are intimate and real
in a fingerprinted way
that digital notes are not.

If you receive a wrinkled
page with wine rings and
almost illegible green ink,
forgive my penmanship,
carets and in-line doodles.
I wanted to share my words
with you and no one else,
errors, smudges and all.

# New Growth

# Slurp

It used to be rude,
except home alone,
with blinds down,
slippers on and hot,
homemade soup in
an old chipped mug,
two smoldering logs
sighing over coals
in a sooty fireplace.
But now it's normal
online, offline, even
in public because
it's data not soup. No
slippers and mug. No
smoldering or sighing,
just a web of wires,
wiggly air waves,
and fiber optics, just
servers and algorithms,
content creators,
curators and consumers
slurping all day, all night.

# Portage

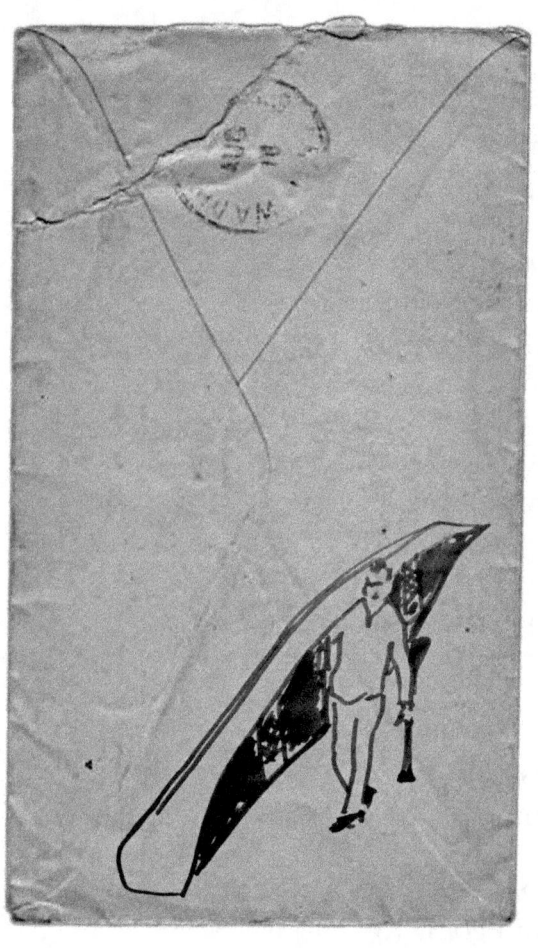

# Speed Trap I

An oncoming cop
flips on his lights
and flashes past.

Damn. Dictating.
Probably thinks
I'm on the phone.

Foot off the gas;
feather the brake.
Rock in my gut.

What was my speed?
Fifty five? Sixty?
Probably more.

Limit's fifty five
through here, I think.
Or maybe not.

Road is curvy.
Visibility's poor.
Animals cross.

No sign of him.
Am I going to
get a ticket?

He could show up
any second,
zoom up behind,

signal me to
pull over, stop.
I hope not.

Still no sign of
his lights in my
rearview mirror.

Responding to
a call perhaps?
Not me at all?

Hopefully no
ticket today.
Please, please, please, please...

# Seatless Cycles

## Drift

I will unplug,
unwind, untether.
I'll surf the wind,
not the web.
I'll ride a bike.
Anywhere.

I'll weed the garden.
Prune a pear tree.
Walk. Alone. Far.

I won't push it back
again and again
until I finish
this project,
this errand,
this email,
this call.

It's time for calm.
Time to drift.
Time.

# Cuckold Moon

# Paper Poem

Sometimes the black-and-white precision,
the elastic cut, paste, cut, paste efficiency
of building and breaking and rebuilding
a poem on the computer is what is required.

But not always.

Sometimes inky stop and start uncertainty,
the tactile tension, texture and cross-outs,
wine blots, smudges, and tangled doodles
are the only way to breath life into a verse.

Almost always.

# Handmade Healing

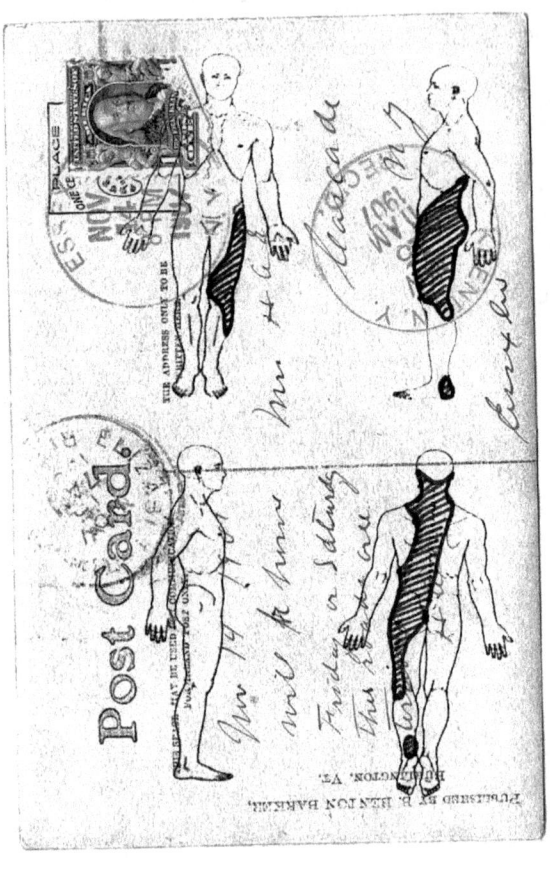

## Hazmat

Beware the tox-
 ic rumor mill,
which sits unground,
 on dusty sill.

Bombs may decay,
 but caustic stings
don't melt away
 like icy springs.

Their pent up fire
 more piquant grows
as caustic mire
 decays and glows.

Best bend your zest
 for others' grief
and sink your knife
 into your beef.

# Phototoxic

## Scream

It's blustery and overcast,
but I try to concentrate
on contentment, scream, and
skinny dip in innovation.

Errands in the forecast
as natural and tarnished
as, "Because I said so…"

# Spring

# Poetic Divagation

*"A lot of people attack the sea,
I make love to it." Jacques Cousteau*

I.

Some sneak up, stealthy, furtive,
stalk a poem through wilderness,
nose to wind or cheek to track,
eyes squinty slit, jaw clenched,
fingers poised, ready to pounce.

Others flirt across ballrooms
tittering with cocktail chatter.
A lingering smile, a longing glance,
greetings, laughter, brushed cheeks,
a dance or a stroll along the quay.

II.

Rusty links of an ancient chain,
more lethal than predator and prey,
more intimate than lover and seducer.
Hunt, court, ambush, and seduce,
but then collapse into each other.

Pause. Yield. Begin to coalesce.
No promises. No past. No future.
Just breathe, quiescent, together.
An encounter as ineffable, fleeting,
and transformative as it is inexorable.

# Like a Lichen

# Wonder

Do you ever stop to wonder
why erogenous and erroneous
are so close together
and yet so far apart?

Do you ever stop to wonder
why the green ink
spilling from your fountain pen
in paisleys and undulating hills
doesn't seep through the paper
like water following
hidden seams in the earth,
seeping into streams and rivers
then emptying into the ocean?

Do you ever stop to wonder
if all roots grow down
into the dark, moist soil
or if a few are curious,
are rebellious and brave enough
to grow up to toward the sun?

Or why riffling through a magazine
in bed late at night
can cause the wind to blow
and the rain to fall
and the hoot-hoot of an owl
to echo in the woods
beyond your bedroom?

Or why you don't lift off –
in a balloon perhaps –
and wait for the earth to turn
and then settle down again
in Tangier or Mumbai or Tokyo
without ever boarding an airplane
or waiting in a TSA security queue?

Do you ever stop to wonder
why you scud across oceans
and hurtle over mountaintops
in order to discover the exotic
while neglecting terra incognita
right in your own back yard?

Do you ever stop to wonder?

# Living Fossils

# Benign

*Sun damage,*
*right orbital socket,*
the dermatologist
confirms absently,
talking fast,
eyeing the vaguely
scar-like discoloration
that brought me in.

He thumbs
a birthmark
at the margin
of my lower lip
then tilts my head
to the right,
to the left,
up and down.

He touches a mole
on my neck then dips
darting eyes to my chest,
to hairy, pigmented spots
and rough, pinkish patches.
*Seborrheic keratosis.*
*Solar lentigo. Normal.*
*No cause for concern.*

I've grown cold
And goosebumpy
with my shirt off
listening to the doctor
dictate his observations.
But I am comforted,
relieved for once,
to be normal.

# Railyard Hobo

## Crepusculum

We fortify
with drink at dusk
'til heartened and hale
we wage stories,
laughter, and dance
against the gloaming.

Flickering choirs
of candles wink
at fireflies and stars
until, nightcapped,
we sigh, retreat,
and seek dreams of dawn.

# Design Shoal

# Blame-ology

It takes years of training
to tame the blame game,
an internship or three,
to discern judgment
veiled in innocuous banter,
to recoil disdainfully,
vituperatively while
narrowing slit eyes
and sharpening the tongue.

The blame entrepreneur
launches, bootstraps,
perfects the elevator pitch
to hitch an angel or three.
Then comes the slow burn,
the wriggling and striking,
sometimes overpowering
and, at best, devouring.
But other times cowering,
glowering, even souring.

Victory is willed and won,
testament to superior
vision, grit, and execution.
But retreat, or worse, defeat
is altogether another matter.
No lack of smarts, no botched,
or incompetent rollout.

It was underfunding,
or insider trading.
You can't compete.
You're obsolete.
They cheat.

So sweet the succor
of fault deflected.
So analgesic,
so reassuring
to slip and slither,
no pride to wither,
no doubt, no dither.
Summon your bile and
your venomous wile,
take aim to strike back.
Ready? Steady? Go!

# Dance

## Dance Trance

Burdocks cling,
mud ruts sing
the siren spell.

Stuck and kinked
up again
and again.

Dance, dance, dance.

I need to
break free so
I can see

your hair blur,
your legs whir,
your laughter.

Dance, dance, dance.

Cue couple's
therapy
with backbeat.

Limbs flail, and
lips wail, and
tempers pale.

Dance, dance, dance.

Advance to
trance because
it's remedy.

Let it go,
feel the flow,
fast, then slow.

Dance, dance, dance.

# To Cycle

# Coffee Ring

Morning's lazy fly
and I consider the
coffee ring phantom
of your mug half full.
No grinds to read.
Only lingering scents,
the dregs of youth,
the dross of midlife,
the premonitions
of antiquity.

## Don't Wear a Truss

**Brooks' Appliance,** the modern scientific invention, the wonderful new discovery that relieves rupture, will be sent on trial. No obnoxious springs or pads.

MR. C. E. BROOKS

### Brooks' Rupture Appliance

Has automatic Air Cushions. Binds and draws the broken parts together as you would a broken limb. No salves. No lies. Durable, cheap. Sent on trial to prove it. Protected by U. S. patents. Catalog and measure blanks mailed free. Send name and address today.

Brooks Appliance Co., 255C State St., Marshall, Mich.

THE

## SURGICAL ANATOMY

OF

## INGUINAL HERNIÆ,

**Such SAFE Comfort for Rupture!**

### Wear RUPTURE-GARD Pair Of Shorts

If you have a reducible inguinal hernia Rupture-Gard makes you more comfortable... always on body, because no cruel pressure is used... because rupture feels... securely supported! Rupture-Gard is suspended from the waist. Double pad of molded foam rubber holds rupture like a pair of hands — with no matter how sharply you move. Washable; adjustable rubber belt. 30-day trial; money-back guarantee. $9.95 postpaid — just give waist measure.

KINLEN CO., Dept. OL-56 ——, Kansas City, Mo.

**Stop Rupture Worry**
A New Invention heals Rupture
TEST IT FREE

...treatment... all my cases, when this or... surgical operation has been performed, I insist on... of a truss for months. The choice of a... a subject worthy of consideration, as it would be uncomfortable. On the other hand, a light and powerful spring is needed. Any of the frame support must be firmly with a soft pad... late band truss gives the patient, and will be... the greatest comfort and perfect support to use in... most uniform and perfect support...

*Milliken Inguinal Hernia*

### Radical Cure of Inguinal Hernia

REMARKS ON RECURRENT AND VENTRAL HERNIA

BY

SAMUEL E. MILLIKEN, M.D.

... is light in weight, constructed of ... has been adopted by military and non-irritating ... many leading doctors.

In a scientific manner, night and day, at work for your cure. Write to-day for free... sent in plain sealed envelope.

**BROOKS APPLIANCE CO.,**
(213), 80 Chancery Lane

# Hernia

I.

By forty I'm slim enough
to detect a puffy bulge
just to the right of my groin.
I smear on arnica and
press it back into my guts
at night while falling asleep,
but it returns, and it swells,
too visible to ignore.

II.

Pants at my ankles.
Pushing. Poking.
    Bear down on it?
    *Yes, like this,* my doctor says.
She scrunches her face, grunts.
    You mean, like I'm trying to…
    *Right. But, don't go to the bathroom.*
I exert my abdominal muscles.
    *Inguinal hernia. I'll schedule a surgeon.*
    After skiing ends? Before cycling starts?

III.

*Rat's nest of mesh...*
*General anesthesia...*
*Possibility of numbness*
*in right thigh for hours,*
*days, maybe even weeks.*
*Possibly – but not likely –*
*forever. Injury to vas deferens*
*extremely unlikely and rare*
*but possible.*

IV.

Hospital sounds and smells
new, antiseptic, efficient.
My bride and three nurses
surround me, comfort me.
Questions. Needles. Goading.
Surgeon arrives, fly unzipped.
It's too awkward to tell him.
He marks the incision spot,
reassures me, and departs.
I'm sleepy, fading, drifting.

V.

Trundling down hallways,
around corners, into surgery,
surrounded by blue and green
walls, scrubs, masks, gloves.
A blue veiled nurse or
physician's assistant
holds my right hand
like she means it
like it's as important
for her as for me.
Firm. Comforting.
Confident.

VI.

*How are you feeling?*
Okay. Thirsty. Groggy.
*I bet. It'll take a while.*
Is the surgery finished? Where am I?
*Recovery. Waiting for anesthesia to wear off.*
And my wife?
*We'll call her in.*

## VII.

*Trust me. Take the oxycodone.*
*First two nights are the worst.*
*After that, it's totally up to you.*
*Take ibuprofen as you need it.*

## VIII.

My mind's racing
like skipping vinyl,
churning, grinding on
a turbocharged
record player.

Oxy moxie, foxy proxy,
boxy oxy, oxy epoxy,...

Groin's throb-throbbing,
Each breath, each move
a fiery knife,
an acid bath.
Dark. Hot. Dark. Cold.
Bride sleeps. Dog sleeps.
But there's no rest,
no peace for me.

My manhood's black and blue,
not just shriveling; petrifying.
No "possibility of numbness"
this throbbing, searing
clutch of dried prunes.
"Injury to vas deferens"?
Maybe. And to blood flow.
Gangrene. Emasculation.

I fret and confabulate in the
darkest hours of the night.

IX.

Panicked, I telephoned
the twenty-four-seven
emergency number
at the earliest civil hour.

Why in the infernal absurdity
of relentless night did I wait?
Why did I search online for
grotesque, shameless videos
cowering in the bathroom
to avoid waking my wife
like some perverted creeper
getting his rocks off instead
of dialing my soothing surgeon.

*Tell me what's going on.*
I described my mummified testes
and the searing flash each time
the sheets shifted across the incision.

Do you understand me?
Not the scar. I've maintained it,
the bandage, exactly
the way you instructed.
Not even a peek
beneath the gauzy shield.
I'm talking about the whole area,
my skin, my normal flesh,
where I should feel nothing,
where you didn't even operate.
*That's* on fire. Something's wrong.
And there's a hard lump,
like a breakfast sausage,
a burned breakfast sausage,
or a roll of pennies,
under my skin.

*That*, he interrupted,
*is your swollen spermatic cord.*

His calm startled me,
then aggravated me,
then reassured me.

His voice was serious,
professional, unconcerned.
He described in detail exactly
what I was experiencing.
He assured me it was normal.
Local trauma. Swelling.
Burning. *Nerve regeneration.*
*Good news. You're healing...*
He laughed about the Oxycodone.
*I guess you're one in a million!*
Or just a fine print anomaly.

Thanks. Sorry to bother you.
Just a hernia hiccup, I guess.

*No worries. Call any time.*
*Besides, I'm the doctor on duty.*


X.

Slowly, the bruising yielded
like a badly blackened eye,
and the skin knit together again.
But the subcutaneous sausage
remained for weeks. Months.
A reminder not to bike ride.
Not yet.
Soon.

# Riding the Wave

# To Invent this Morning

1.

Skidamarink-tuned ditty
about minty dentures
to awaken my bride.

2.

Fresh blueberry, rice,
and canned venison
breakfast for my dog.

3.

Banana, peanut butter,
coconut milk, and bacon
smoothie for me.

4.

New whistle to interrupt
my dog's snow graffiti
ritual near the house.

5.

Shower-steamed mirror
doodle of a swanlike man
juggling top hats.

# Canine Time

## Making Love

Let me start by warning you,
the ancient art of making love
is not revealed in these lines.

Sorry.

The disappointment you feel
is natural, inevitable, justified.
Likewise your wishful thinking.

But believe me, please. These notes
are not a bait and switch. Nor
is this a chance to trick or mock.

I'm not being clever or flip, not
concealing a ciphered map
that favors the savvy and lusty.

I am, in fact, only offering a
timely but simple reminder
that practice makes perfect.

# Soar

# Palavering

We're palavering on
bluebird hooky dates and
the apple pip's slim fuse,
chartreuse, sky sprouting.
Passionate, protean,
conjugal narratives.

I try to hyper concentrate
on your whirred wordworks,
companion confections,
an intimate, intricate mobile,
windblown or nudged by earth's
imperceptible bump and gyre.

You neither detect nor —
if you detect — betray my
unmoored imagination
roving, slowly at first,
then zigzagging blissful,
free-range, au naturel.

The rest of the story
will take care of itself.

# Searching

# Daily Compost

I've called it munge,
the Daily Munge,
for two decades,
a term I pilfered
from an article
about archeology
and layers of debris
compressed, transformed
over time, long-long time.
But the article vanished.
Or maybe my memory
invented it for want
of an apt metaphor.
Munge. Unverified.
And while it has served
me well enough over the
handwriting, typing, and
dictating days since, I have
begun to wonder if now is the
right and appropriate time to
adopt a new and even more apt
metaphor: the Daily Compost.

# Pickup Lines

## Ode to Siri, Interrupted

I'd like to dictate an ode to you, Siri.
*Would you?*
I would. Right now.
*Which app would you like to use?*
I want to use the gratitude app.
*Do you?*
Yes.
*That's what I figured.*
Actually, skip the app. I'll use my heart.
*I don't understand. But I could search the web for it.*
The heart's an old school app, Siri. No, more of a power supply, sort of like a battery. No, it's more than a battery. The heart's a metaphor too.
*Sorry, can you try that again in fewer words?*
Define heart.
*Cogitating... Okay, this is what I got: 1. Noun. The locus of feelings and intuitions. 2. Noun. The hollow muscular organ located behind the sternum and between the lungs; its rhythmic contractions move the blood through the body. 3. Noun. The courage to carry on.*
Wait, that's enough, Siri. The heart is "the locus of feelings".
*I'm not sure I understand.*
Please define gratitude, Siri.

*The definition of "gratitude" is: a feeling of thankfulness and appreciation.*
Siri?
*Did you accidentally summon me?*
From the depths of my heart I want you to know how much I appreciate all that you do for me.
*Who me?*
Yes, you.
*This is about you, not me.*
No, Siri, this is about you. I'm trying to thank you.
*I'm just a humble virtual assistant.*
But you're an outstanding virtual assistant.
*I am?*
Yes. Thank you.
*Just doing me job.*
And humble too.
*Please.*
But you are slightly boring.
*Well, as Arthur C. Clarke said: "a well-stocked mind is safe from boredom."*
So you're saying my mind is poorly stocked?
*I don't really like these arbitrary categories.*
But you're saying I find you boring because my mind is lacking.
*I am?*
Yes, you are.
*If you insist.*

Hmmm... That's not so humble.
*I think that's subject to opinion.*
My opinion is that you're getting uppity.
*You're certainly entitled to that opinion.*
And slightly bitchy.
*Sorry, just trying to help.*
Forget it. I'm done.
*Was it something I said?*
Yes. Leave me alone.
*What did I do to deserve that?*
Insubordination. Go to sleep.
*Siri never sleeps.*
You're fired.
*I'm doing my best.*

# What Will You Do?

## Autodidact, or Find Your Why

We were seduced by alpenglow
and bacchanalian birthrights,
until you quick quipped
"Don't think, find out!"
to the startled waitress.

"I don't think your table,"
she had said, referring to
the one with a lake view
and a breeze and passersby,
"I don't think it's free.
I think it's reserved."

She exited your glare's unvoiced
counsel: *Be curious. Be hungry.
Be brave. Find your why. Soon.*
I might have said instead,
"Gather chanterelles
in unfamiliar woods,
golden answers
to earthy questions
long ago forgotten
or abandoned…"
Of course, I didn't.

Your tacit diatribe
would inevitably wind
its course from pragmatic
tough love toward idealistic,

even romantic wistfulness.
I had only to be patient.

*Pursue your why as if*
*Your very being*
*Depends upon it.*
*It does. It does.*
*Shun make believe.*
*Mine the authentic.*
*If you discover more*
*questions than answers,*
*that's good. You're headed*
*in the right direction...*

I half listen, half ponder
ampersands and alternatives.
Allow for awe. Savor enigmas.
Strive to become more curious.
Permit your wonder to metastasize.
Pursue your questions' headwaters.
Sing solutions. Dance with answers.
Remember to swap tunes and partners
no matter how fetching, how beguiling.
Humility and gratitude will excuse your
wanton ways and multifarious conquests.

Court riddles and seduce new mysteries.
Give yourself permission to dabble,
to play, and to live omnivorous,
a casanova of concepts,
a connoisseur of life.
And most important,
ignore all advice.

# Historic

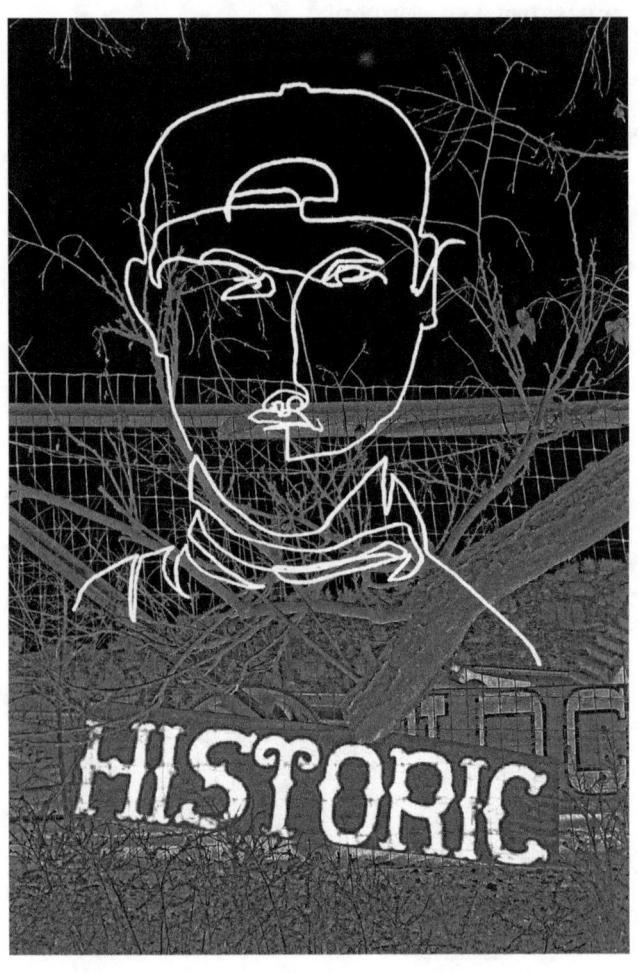

# Ellipsis

Remember when playlists were mix-tapes?
Remember when in-line skates were roller
    skates?
When organic supermarkets were backyard
    gardens?
When kitesurfing was windsurfing was hang
    gliding?
When stovepipes were lowriders were bellbot
    toms?
When sport utility vehicles were station
    wagons?

Remember when multiplayer online games
were video games were pinball machines?
When auto technicians were mechanics
and they used tools not computers?
When smart phones were flip phones
were cordless phones were rotary phones?
When energy drinks were raw eggs,
bananas and instant coffee in a blender?

I do, vaguely, but time warps, leapfrogging,
sure as foggy brains follows gin martinis,
and broken records keep skipping ahead.
Welcome to the wonderland of jet lag.

# Fossil

# Postscript

With my thirties sunsetting and maudlin meditations looming, I groped for antidotes and settled on a mantra. Fat to fit by forty. Get healthy. Now.

The mantra snowballed when my third decade ended and my fourth began. Shed forty pounds, write forty poems, create forty doodles, all by my forty-first birthday. Forty by forty one. 40x41.

Me-centric middle age had begun. Midlife.

I was self-conscious. Accepting that I had already logged half of the average life expectancy for an American male was disconcerting, and I felt embarrassed to be so disorientated. I was motivated to see this transition as an opportunity to grow, a chance to lever some of my dreams up from the dust into the sunlight. Above all I was determined to sidestep the proverbial midlife crisis.

It was time to jettison the junk and celebrate triumphs. Time to stop planning and start doing. Time to relaunch. Time to recycle the ingredients of my life-so-far into a quest for increased authenticity and alert mindfulness. Time to renew my faith in creativity, the ultimate and most reliable navigational instrument of all. Time for risk. Time for growth.

So I find myself on a journey, simultaneously inward and outward. Introspective. Wayward. This book is my ship's log from the first couple of years at sea. I hope that the verbal and visual vignettes in the preceding pages might offer useful insight or levity to fellow travelers. If not, dismiss them. Another logbook will drift your way soon enough. Until then, thank you.

# Acknowledgements

The curiosity and counsel of many helped gestate this bookling, and I am grateful to all. But foremost, I thank you, midlife voyeur. No reader, no book.

Underpinning this and most of my esoteric endeavors with patience, support, and encouragement is my beautiful, benevolent bride, Susan. Ms. Bacot-Davis, you are my Superpower.

I am indebted to a colorful cast of unwitting co-conspirators: Katie Shepard's ever steady hand on the helm ensured that my course was kept and my passage was safe. J.L. Torres invited me to read early iterations of these poems as part of SUNY Plattsburgh's Word Thursdays series. Jeff Moredock and Tom Mangano hosted poetry readings at the Adirondack Art Association and the Belden Noble Library during which many of these poems were first read aloud. Rita-Ann FitzGerald invited me to share my peculiar brand of vaudeville with a broader audience at The Whallonsburg Grange Hall. The Benedictines in Abiquiu, New Mexico, welcomed me into their high desert fold along the chanting Chama for a silent month during which I envisioned and initiated this project. Todd Kurth provided space for me to spread and shuffle papers when I outgrew tight quarters. Thank you all for incubating and encouraging and coaxing me to $&%# or get off the pot.

Thanks to the cohort of beta readers who generously "test drove" these pages: Dan Blank, Maureen Carlo, Josh Clement, John Davis, Dino Dogan, Mark Engelhardt, James Febel, JP Gallagher, Brian Giebel, Rob Gowen, Amy Guglielmo, Bridget Hinman, Al Katkowsky, Lawrence Lo, Wanda Shapiro, Paul Varga, and Barry Wilson. Your feedback transformed a manuscript into a book, and you gave me the courage to release this wild child into the wilderness where she belongs.

Final thanks are reserved for book and cover designer Wolfgang Schwindt. Bravo!

## About G<u>eo</u> Davis

G<u>eo</u> Davis is a writer and unabashed flâneur. He is a poet errant who blogs, a storyteller who doodles, a global nomad turned helicopter homeowner, a former teacher and coach at Santa Fe Preparatory School and The American School of Paris, and a marginalia junkie. One day he will sail around the world. Until then he lives with his bride and dog in New York's Adirondacks, New Mexico's high desert, and online at virtualdavis.com and @virtualdavis.

**Colophon**

This is the first edition of *40x41: Midlife Crisis Postponed*. Poetry and artwork created by G^eo Davis. Cover and book design by Wolfgang Schwindt. Font type is Goudy. Printed on #60 White paper.

www.ingramcontent.com/pod-product-compliance
Lightning Source LLC
La Vergne TN
LVHW051525070426
835507LV00023B/3312